Count The Monster Trucks!

This Book Belongs To:

_____

Your child loves monster trucks?

At the end of the book, please find our e-mail address to send us an e-mail, and we will send you completely free monster truck coloring pages, that every toddler would be sure to enjoy! Simply write "Yes, I want to receive free monster truck coloring pages!" and we will send them to you, completely for free! The coloring pages are in printable PDF format.

Copyright © By: Jasper Daesdonk Publishing

All right reserved. No part of this publication may be reproduced, distributed, or transmitted in any form or by any means, including photocopying, recording, or other electronic or mechanical methods, without the prior written permission of the publisher, except in the case of brief questions embodied in critical reviews and certain other noncommercial use permitted by copyright law.

Count all the monster trucks like this one! ➡

Congratulations! You guessed correctly

There were 3 such monster trucks in the picture

Count all the monster trucks like this one! ➡

Congratulations! You guessed correctly

There were 5 such monster trucks in the picture

Find 2 of the same monster trucks!

Congratulations! You guessed correctly

Here are 2 of the same monster trucks

Count all the monster trucks like this one!

Congratulations! You guessed correctly

There were 2 such monster trucks in the picture

Are there more of these  or these  monster trucks?

Congratulations! You guessed correctly

There were more of these

x4

x3

Count all the monster trucks like this one! ➡

Congratulations! You guessed correctly

There was 1 such monster truck in the picture

Count all the monster trucks like this one!

Congratulations! You guessed correctly

There were 4 such monster trucks in the picture

Count how many of the same monster trucks are on this page!

Congratulations! You guessed correctly

There were 5 of the same monster trucks on that page

Count all the monster trucks like this one! ➡

Congratulations! You guessed correctly

There were 6 such monster trucks in the picture

Count all the monster trucks like this one! ➡️

Congratulations! You guessed correctly

There were 2 such monster trucks in the picture

Are there more of these  or these  monster trucks?

Congratulations! You guessed correctly

There were more of these

x2

x1

Count all the monster trucks like this one!

Congratulations! You guessed correctly

There were 8 such monster trucks in the picture

Count all the monster trucks like this one! ➡

Congratulations! You guessed correctly

There was 1 such monster truck in the picture

Count all the monster trucks like this one!

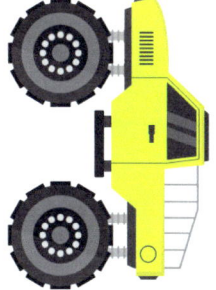

Congratulations! You guessed correctly

There were 3 such monster trucks in the picture

Find 2 of the same monster trucks!

Congratulations! You guessed correctly

Here are 2 of the same monster trucks

Count all the monster trucks like this one! ➡

Congratulations! You guessed correctly

There were 7 such monster trucks in the picture

Count all the monster trucks like this one! ➡

Congratulations! You guessed correctly

There were 4 such monster trucks in the picture

Are there more of these 🚚 or these 🚚 monster trucks?

Congratulations! You guessed correctly

There were more of these

 x5

 x2

Count all the monster trucks like this one! ➡

Congratulations! You guessed correctly

There were 10 such monster trucks in the picture

I AM VERY GRATEFUL YOU PURCHASED THIS BOOK. I HOPE YOU AND YOUR CHILD SPEND AN UNFORGETTABLE TIME HAVING FUN AND LEARNING TOGETHER FROM THIS BOOK.

IF YOU CAN, I WOULD BE EXTREMELY GRATEFUL IF YOU COULD LEAVE A REVIEW ON AMAZON. WE ARE A SMALL FAMILY BUSINESS AND DEPEND ON REVIEWS TO REACH MORE FAMILIES.

THANK YOU AGAIN FOR YOUR PURCHASE AND YOUR TRUST. I HOPE YOU ENJOY YOUR BOOK AND HAVE A GREAT TIME WITH YOUR FAMILY

HAVE A NICE DAY!

WE HOPE THE BOOK HAS MET YOUR EXPECTATIONS. IF YOU FOUND ANY MISTAKES IN THE BOOK, PLEASE CONTACT US BY EMAIL, AND WE WILL CORRECT THEM AS SOON AS POSSIBLE

office.dannyd@gmail.com

INDEPENDENTLY PUBLISHED

Jasper Daesdonk Publishing

Made in the USA
Columbia, SC
16 November 2023